The Silence That Spoke

Mona

BookLeaf Publishing

India | USA | UK

Made with ❤ on the BookLeaf Publishing Platform
www.bookleafpub.in
www.bookleafpub.com

Dedication

To all those who understood my silence —
and to those who misunderstood it.
This book wouldn't exist without either.

Preface

Silence - sometimes mistaken for peace, other times for distance. For me, it has never been just the absence of words — instead it has been a language of its own. It has raged, wept, healed, and screamed within me. And slowly, quietly, it began to write itself.

This book is a collection of those whispers — poems born in the stillness of long nights, between unsaid apologies and unspoken longings, amid quiet anguish and loud heartbreaks.

The poems you'll find here are not meant to be understood in one sitting. Some may resonate immediately, others might wait patiently in the back of your mind until life makes them clearer.

I hope this book becomes a quiet companion, the kind that doesn't interrupt but stays with you when the world gets too loud.

-Mona

Acknowledgements

Thank you to those who heard me in silence, believed in me in a scattered world,
and held my voice when I couldn't.

Words are but a chaos
in the subtle world of silence.

Known to many,
fathomed by a few!

From a melting candle,
to a shattered glass
he has come a long way, alas!

Broken pieces, glued together, make art.
A prettier version of the original heart...
"People say so"!

He still wonders, is it truly though?

When no words of love
seep through the hard-hearty walls of his inner cove,
he looks at himself in the mirror
and sees not a man... but a cold, still stone... err.

Waves of affection
and tempests of rage

someday, they're bound
to flee the shores

'tis folly to siege
what won't be chained in a cage.

Sometimes I wonder,
what keeps me from you.

sometimes I wonder,
what keeps you from me.

Silence consoles my quest!

and, my heart wanders
yet again!

My shadow burdens me
with Reality!
My reality sucks the life out of me
with insanity!

And yet, here I am,
looking at your face,
And smiling like an idiot...
EVERY SINGLE DAY!

Should I wait
or should I look out?

Should I keep patience
or must I freak out?

For,
the long road,
to the everlasting...

Lies right in front of my eyes
and yet far off reach

Should I walk up to him,
or I wait again...

For this is a circle of
summer and rain.

She kept screaming
with swollen eyes,
and tightly shut lips.

He kept hearing,
for as long as she remembers .

Someone asked her, who are you?

"Painted like words,
on a black & white canvas!"
She answered as her cherry red lips smiled...

I am a pretty good girl
sitting in the sunshine
wanting to feel like a neurotic villain.

Isn't that the perfect prelude to mayhem!

Hundreds of stories,
seal my lips!

Suffocating me, breathing heavily
drastically trying... to escape.
To tell the world,
who I really am.

But I am too good
at embodying the scars,
and tolerate
in utter silence!

I forgave her,
yes... I took a deep breath
and, I forgave her!

For the scars she gave me,
for the person she made me
yet...
she ain't forgotten ...

The first thing I see
when I close my eyes,
and it's dark outside!

Is the Red colour
of your eyes
and of your lips.
The pain in my heart,
that silently dwells
and
the Drop of blood
dripping out of yours!!!

A loner's heart
an empty heart
no desire
just fire... fire

Cry cry
tears leave the eye
just to dry... dry

A loner's soul
the only soul
oh, how he would console.
The loner's heart
his own heart
the empty heart
no desire... just fire fire

I couldn't sleep that night,
though my bed was soft and tight,
my thoughts were still, the room was right—
yet sleep stayed out of sight.

And then I heard, so soft, so slight,

A cricket singing through the night.
A tiny voice, a secret song,
from his small world to where I belong.

Silence — an eerie presence,
constant, unwavering, and supreme.
But she remained oblivious to it...
until it came hauntingly close.

An accident barred her,
from listening to what life sounds like.
Only then she realised,
indeed, how life sounds like.

In all that blunt silence,
she could finally hear her beating heart,
the occasional radio static,
and everything else
that usually got lost in the day-to-day chatter.

She chose to dwell where fireflies
would burn and soar through starry skies,
each night they danced in silent streams,
forsaking all their daylight dreams.

They shimmered in the haunted gloom,
of wild woods wrapped in a whispered blume*

A dream it was — but still, she'd run,
to chase the night, to be the one.

*German word for 'flower'

Shadows have been a dear friend
& Silence the obvious comfort.
Left with barely any memory of a colourful past -
I stand on the verge of a half-life
spent, spellbound in a strange cast.
-

But vigorous & fiery to break-free
I am here to rule,
& surrender to a universe
that invites me to unshackle.

Choose with care what stays behind,
let memory be - silent, gentle, kind.
Hold close the warmth, the light, the song,
and leave the rest where it belongs.

Yes, you heard it — not to forget,
but to forgive the scars we met.
For bitter stains on golden years
deserve neither anger, nor our tears.

Cradle the good, release the pain—
and cleanse the heart that dares remain.
In every echo, in every sigh,
choose love to keep, and let wounds fly.

Silence has no tongue, no voice,
no borders, no divided choice.
Yet somehow, it's misunderstood—
by hearts that never truly could.

No words, no lines to cross or spell
and still, it builds an unseen shell.
What should I call it? Strange defiance?
or simply... the irony of silence?

She was disappointed —
with the world,
with the one she loved,
but most of all,
with herself.

Dressed in satin, finest hue,
adorned with pearls that softly grew,
beneath a starry, glittering sky,
she stood alone — no reason why.
Crickets chirped in the distant dark,
eerie silence left its mark.

That's when he came — adorned by a scar
in shadowed steel — a blacked-out car.
He saw the tears, the bitter eyes,
no words, just glances — sharp, precise.
He gestured gently; she stepped inside,
as if the night could turn the tide.

An hour passed, the city near,
their breaths were heavy, brushed with fear.
Yet somehow, safe — they'd found a thread
in silence, where all else had fled.

He dropped her home, no words, no plea,
just glances shared — too raw, too free.
and there it ended, soft and bare—
a love story... brief as midnight air.

She was naïve,
peeking through unfamiliar eyes —
searching for signs of madness,
of chaos cloaked in disguise.

When instead she was the One!
Engulfing a freakshow
& yet, Silently smiling like
the morning was still bright
& every night was beaming with moonlight.

The night was loud...
her ears couldn't bear
the cacophony of silence!

Here we sit — silent, still,
together, chasing a fleeting thrill.
Feeling peaceful,
in our own little ways
smiling at each other
and yet,
I am looking at the horizon
while you
patiently await the conclusion!

Try to be Silent
just for a moment
& experience,
how chaos makes one feel
impeccably peaceful!

When the faded sun
creeps through the drapes,
& the periwinkles bloom
outside the window panes

The world around me
seems so peaceful & serene
until i remember
the storm that grows within
& just waiting to blast out
layered carefully under my
naked skin!

When the wind blew through her hair,
& the rain drops touched her skin, that was bare.
She felt alive,
like never before.
Her heart beat faster,
& Eyes gleamed.
She took a leap,
and, chose her path,
she carved her own destiny.
When the world kept shutting her,
Yelling
"This isn't your place to be"
She sat in silence, and mumbled,
"This... will never be enough for me"
She rose high & above,
took a flight...
just like...
that frightened little grey dove.

I prefer to communicate
a thousand words,
& a million emotions
with silence.

When a heart breaks, it makes no sound,
no crashing noise, no echoes around.

Other than the occasional
softest murmur of a tear droplet,
that keeps falling on the cheeks...

Some days it weeps in quiet grief,
other days... it sighs in relief.

The circle of life stays incomplete
till you've lived each shade — bitter and sweet.
Not just seen, but let them be,
embraced their quiet intensity.

Like friendship — it's not just made
of laughter in the light of day,
but proven when you choose to stay
through silent storms that come your way.

Have you ever stayed awake all night,
breathing in stardust,
falling softly
through a clear sky's light?
The infinite twinkle of cosmic beings —
so mighty, so far —
is quietly hushed
by the silence of stars.
They surrender,
without a sound,
to the vastness
that wraps them all around.
Isn't it mesmerising?

"I am a destroyer,"
said the violent confessor,
surrounded by debris —
emotions,
and unused magical potions.
"I am a destroyer...
and now, I submit.
I gave my soul,
my final breath — every bit."
Then silence spreads,
in amber light,
through dusty haze,
a fleeting ache,
a waiting phase...
until everything
goes storming again.

She still had his number
saved in her phone...
the one who had left,
leaving memories alone—
some sweet, some sour,
her soul, her desire,
her everything—
gone in an hour.
It's been almost two years...
yet, she still dials that line,
listens intently to a voice
frozen in time.
A digital ghost,
no warmth, no breath—
just:
"Record your message after the beep."
She sobs instead,
in that silent sweep—
where all she hears
is nothingness,
and a grief that doesn't sleep.

The mountain dwellers
pay homage to the gone,
with coloured flags that whisper prayers—
each one, a name they lean upon.
Placed high near peaks,
in clusters of 108
as if to help the soul ascend,
untethered by fate.
It rises then,
beyond the realm of form—
drifting through valleys,
unbothered by storm.
It rustles the leaves
where silence is deep,
and continues to wander,
without pause, without sleep—
a soft, unseen flight
toward the ever-awaiting light.

She was looking gorgeous that day,
her nose pin softening her face,
cherry-red lips,
extra delicious in their grace.
Eagerly, she sat in front of him,
twirling hair between her fingers,
her earrings shimmered,
soft chimes that lingered.
-

He was flabbergasted,
exhausted,
agitated—
tainted by the sweat of the day.
He blasted off to his bae,
about everything that went wrong today...
she sat there, listening silently,
holding back tremors,
as far as she could, quietly.

The valley looked extra serene,
from my tiny wooden window,
the wind, with quiet grace,
greeted me like a friendly fellow.
Little hanging bells,
chimed their soft refrain,
announcing the wind's arrival,
in silence, once again.

Her favorite crockery set
shattered into pieces—
but her ears couldn't hear
the breaking releases.
Their rattling relationship
took up all the space -
leaving them to scream
in silence seeking a simple solace!

Over the years,
she accumulated a dozen letters,
pouring her heart onto the pages,
spreading words carefully—at dusk, at dawn.
She kept speaking through them,
but never had the courage to send.
Until one day,
all that silence was locked within,
and she had nothing more to say.

They were born without a voice—
yet none could ever tell.
Their tongues had their own language:
to talk,
to touch,
to tempt…
each night,
they met in wordless flame,
entwined in a steamy, sultry game—
a silent affair,
too loud to name.

Could stillness stir a storm inside?
Could chaos come with peace as guide?
Can silence echo louder than sound?
Can a single grain of sand, feel heavier than the palm
that holds it?

The irony lies not in the claim—
but in the heart that feels the flame.

I don't want to be blamed
for the wreckage you become.

Hence, never question
my silence ever again.
You are not built to
survive my chaos.

www.ingramcontent.com/pod-product-compliance
Lightning Source LLC
Chambersburg PA
CBHW070609160726
48003CB00005B/2191